The Ministry of Marriage

(Set Up for Failure?)

Tools for a Successful Marriage Within the Body of Christ

The Ministry of Marriage

(Set Up for Failure?)

Tools for A Successful Marriage Within the Body of Christ

Mirielle Archange Gordon

Printed in the United States of America

First Printing, 2023

ISBN: 979-8-218-96454-2

Editor: Iris M. Williams

MAG Publishing
PO Box 411
Lovejoy GA 30228
www.magpublishing.net

Dedication

For my children Christina, Patrick, Abigail, and Malachi,

who one day may be called to this Ministry, may this book be your guide.

"Unless the Lord Build the House,
those who build it labor in vain.
Unless the lord watches over the city,
the watchman stays awake in vain."
(Psalm 127:1)

Table of Contents

*"So shall they fear the name of the Lord from the west, and his glory
from the rising of the sun. When the enemy shall come in like a flood,
the Spirit of the Lord shall lift up a standard against him."*
(Isaiah 59:19)

Foreword

As a person who has experienced multiple divorces, I was drawn to this book from the start. I am so grateful that God commissions authors such as Mirielle to minister to the broken areas of our lives. This book absolutely does that.

I knew that a major part of the reason my marriages didn't work is because of how I viewed myself, but it honestly never occurred to me that my view of the institution of marriage was faulty as well.

Marriage as a ministry?

The thought never entered my mind! Perhaps it hasn't entered yours either.

Mirielle's book will arm you with new perspectives, practical advice, and tools you can use to experience a successful relationship.

The Ministry of Marriage can assist readers in confirming if called to marriage and is an eye-opening message that can help singles avoid a failed relationship. It can also prove beneficial to divorcees by healing the stigma, frustration, and confusion of multiple divorces.

Most importantly, this book can guide church leaders as they prepare singles for marriage.

Iris M. Williams

Welcome

Acknowledgment(s)

I would like to thank my Lord and savior Jesus The Christ for gracing me to use my life experiences to help the body of Christ.

Thank you to my lifelong friend, Lunise Couamin, and my daughter Abigail (who together tagged team me), for never allowing me to stop pushing, and who were constantly encouraging me to keep writing to share this vital message to the body of Christ.

May this book empower YOU to fight the good fight of faith in YOUR marriage.

Remember Jesus loves YOU and so do I.

Mirielle Archange Gordon

Preface

"If the body of Christ fails to acknowledge marriage as a ministry and exercise preventative care, couples are set up for failure." Mirielle Archange Gordon

Married and divorced multiple times, Mirielle Archange Gordon experienced firsthand the associated consequences of heartbreak, societal stigma, and feelings of failure and frustration. Instead of wallowing in pity, she not only decided to seek the wise counsel of the Holy Spirit and research why divorce was so prevalent, but also search for answers to what could be done to change this shattering trend.

Her findings weren't surprising. Studies show that the main reasons couples divorce center around an inability to communicate, money issues, cheating and a lack of skills needed to resolve conflict. Divorce is not only detrimental to the couple but can have a negative impact on children as well causing sadness and even a decrease in their success in school.

We know all too well the problem. But what is the solution?

Mirielle is convinced that premarital counseling and preparation are vital to the sustainability of a healthy, happy, and fruitful marriage. The realization that marriage is a ministry is vital to successful unions among the body of Christ.

"It is my prayer," the author asserts, "that my experience and revelation help the body of Christ revisit their approach to marriage by raising the standard by which couples enter this covenant. Through a variety of methods (including marital retreats, marriage counseling and therapy), I believe couples can strengthen and even repair their union. As a multiple divorcee, I know firsthand how difficult marriage can be if it isn't entered into with the correct mindset, knowledge, and support."

Chapter One:

A Case for Pre-Marital Preparation

The first time we saw premarital preparation was in the garden of Eden where God prepared a home for Adam (**Genesis 1:25**). God created rivers for water to drink, trees, plants for food, and animals. Along with the task for Adam to name the animals, God tasked Adam and Eve to be fruitful and multiply [*minister*] (**Genesis 1:28:31**).

If God instituted marriage, the life joined journey of one man and one woman (**Genesis 2:24**), why is the divorce rate in the church at such an all-time high? I believe the church has done away with the pre aspect (proper preparation) of marriage. The Church overlooked the marriage manual (the Bible) and went straight to operations (wedding ceremonial preparation). God even made provision to ensure people would be able to communicate as evident by the phrase, "Let us make man in our image" (**Genesis 1:26**). This act of God provided men and women with the ability to reason, communicate thoughts and ideas. The ability to reason and solve problems is one of the things that separate humans from animals.

Within the body of believers, there are more people in their second and third marriages than ever before. As a woman, mother of five, and wife on my third marriage, I have identified that one of the contributing factors of this dilemma is poor preparation in the pre-marital stage. The Church has done a phenomenal job sustaining the *idea* of this great institution but has fallen short of proclaiming that marriage is a ministry and providing standards by which one can (or should) enter this covenant in a manner that promotes sustainability.

In theory, we understand that marriage and family are the fabric of our community. In fact, studies have shown crime and community instability can be linked to areas with large populations of single parent homes.

The Lord God instituted the fivefold ministry (five roles that God has called Christians to fill) which advances the Kingdom of God. "God gave some to be apostle; and some prophets; and some evangelist; and some, pastors, and teachers." (**Ephesians 4:11-13**). The criteria to serve in either of these roles is often stringent. For example, to become a minister (holding the position of one of the fivefold ministries), you must go through years of theology school, preceptorship of a reputable church, and prove yourself to be a model or refined citizen of society.

According to the word of God, any person holding a position in one of the fivefold ministries who is unable to manage their home (i.e., unruly children for example) is unfit for that ministry. In the word of God, that minister must first tend to his or her home and then be allowed to minister in the church (**1 Timothy 3:4-5**).

Although the roles of the fivefold ministry are important, none are more significant than the call to be a spouse. God views marriage in such a high standard, He compares His relations to believers as unto the marriage between one man and one woman. In the word of God, "... husbands are to love their wives as Christ loves the Church" (**Ephesians 5:25-27**). Yet the Church (by evidence of action) has seemingly regarded the ministry of marriage as one of lesser importance. However, unlike the criteria for the fivefold ministry, to enter marriage, men and women need only be eighteen years old, have no living un-dissolved marriages, be a member of a Church, and sit through a few days of pre-marital counseling!

Growing up in the church of God, it was embedded in the mind of young people that the one major requirement for marriage was to pray and ensure that your intended was a fellow believer. I often heard the preacher teach from the pulpit that husbands were the head of their wives, wives were to be submissive to their husbands and both were to pray. This would ensure the marriage would be well.

Not only does the church fail to emphasize the fact that marriage is a ministry to which not everyone is called (some people are called to be single until the day they die (**Matthew 19:11-21 MSG**), but we were also not encouraged to obtain training in the vital areas of communication, finance, parenting, and conflict resolution. And we were especially not informed that unrealistic expectations were something that had to die in marriage.

When a family is pregnant, the government offers parenting classes and newborn stress training classes to ensure the success of that parent child relationship. Marriage is no less important than giving birth, but unless we are well trained and informed in the pre-marital stage, marriage in the body of Christ will continue to be a set up for failure.

Imagine if a new convert, a person who just accepted Jesus Christ, requested to pastor a Church. The Church leaders would *never* allow such a reckless act. The leaders would rightfully show that person they are not ready. That new convert would have to sit under years of training as mentioned earlier (**2Timothy 2:14-15 NKJV**).

Why then do leaders of the body of Christ, allow two people without a calling or training in vital areas of communication, finance, parenting, and conflict resolution to come and request to enter the ministry of marriage? Marriage vows are pledged and sealed with the words 'till death do us part.'

It is irresponsible of the Church to allow this practice to continue. We have a Church filled with divorced women and men, broken homes, and hurting children. Husbands who are unable to steward their marriage contributes to absent, frustrated men in the Church. The word of God says when a husband mistreats his wife, his prayer is hindered (**1Peter 3:7**). A frustrated man whose prayers are hindered is less likely to attend Church. This crisis leads to a weakened Church. Preventative care is key. The Church must raise the standard for marriage and re-marriage.

It is important to mention here that people who have been married before tend to believe they do not have to go through an in-depth premarital program for the second marriage. They consider themselves 'experienced.' However, the evidence of the third and fourth marriages has proven that it is a faulty way of thinking. On the contrary, couples reattempting marriage require more training.

Couples reattempting marriage should be recommended to go through a period of therapeutic healing, to assist the individual overcome the trauma, heartache, and fear of failure, among other residue of a broken marriage (dream). This individual should now incorporate the learning in the form of class and or session of how to (if applicable) manage a blended household. If children were involved in the previous marriage, a brief overview on co-parenting may be added for these individuals in the 'parenting class' sessions of the premarital program.

I remember after my separation from my first husband, we struggled and suffered unnecessary verbal altercations over co-parenting. We argued over how much input the new stepparent should have in the parenting process. For example, my eldest daughter was about nine years old and had thick, long natural hair. I did not believe in using relaxers in Childrens hair, despite how difficult it was at times to manage her hair.

Well, my daughter would spend every summer with her father. One summer her stepmother decided to relax her hair. It was infuriating. My poor handling of the situation and my ex-husband and I's failure to establish healthy boundaries (including learning how to co-parent), caused unnecessary trauma to our daughter. It would take many years and therapy for my eldest daughter to overcome that trauma.

This may sound extreme; however, marriage is an extreme ministry, that if not managed correctly can even cause one to lose one's life through suicide (despair), or homicide, (inability to cope with the feeling of failure/loss). In Orlando Florida, a pastor who called himself a prophet fatally shot his wife. (PASTOR WHO CALLS HIMSELF 'THE PROPHET' FATALLY SHOOTS WIFE AT ORLANDO WORKPLACE, POLICE SAY [WESH.COM]) In the news it was presumed one of the reasons this might have taken place was the pastor's inability to cope with the failure of his marriage. **(PASTOR "SYLVESTER OFORI" IN-LAW REVEAL BARBARA TOMMEY 'SUSPECTED MURDER' GIST AS DEM ANNOUNCE BURIAL ARRANGEMENT - BBC NEWS PIDGIN)** In retrospect,, a person reattempting marriage has all the incentives to participate in a premarital program.

On these next few pages take some time to think about/respond to the prompts 'now.' Later, (six months or more) come back and think about/respond to the same prompts. Note how (if applicable) your responses changed.

For Thought: A Case for Pre-Marital Preparation (Now)

How important is preparation for marriage? How should you prepare for marriage?

Which role of the fivefold ministry have you been called? How do you know?

What type of preparation have you had for ministry and/or marriage? Do you feel it was adequate? Why or why not?

What expectations should be considered unrealistic in marriage? Explain your answer.

What are the consequences of low standards in life and marriage?

"The earth is full of the goodness of the Lord." Psalm 31

"I will bless the Lord at all times." Psalm 34

"Take delight in the Lord, and he will give you the desires of your heart." Psalm 37:4

For thought: A Case for Pre-Marital Preparation (Later)

How important is preparation for marriage? How should you prepare for marriage?

Which role of the fivefold ministry have you been called? How do you know?

What type of preparation have you had for ministry and/or marriage? Do you feel it was adequate? Why or why not?

What expectations should be considered unrealistic in marriage? Explain your answer.

What are the consequences of low standards in life and marriage?

"The Lord is kind and merciful." Psalm 103

"Except the Lord build the house, they labour in vain that build it." Psalm 127:1

"Cause me to hear they lovingkindness in the morning; for in thee do I trust." Psalm 143.8

Chapter Two

A Call to Serve

As I mentioned in chapter one, I am in my third marriage. Although many factors contributed to the failure of my two previous marriages, the one factor I will focus on (because it is relevant to the book) is poor preparation during the pre-marital stage.

I was 24 and the mother of a beautiful five-year-old daughter when I married the first time. The condition in which I was to be wed was rushed so that the shame of having a child out of wedlock could be lifted. I was fearful due to the lack of preparation before the marriage.

"Even if you have to live under a bridge," Deacon Fanfan said to me, "it is better to be married and go to heaven than be unmarried and risk going to hell."

My boyfriend at the time and I were young and eager to please God, so we listened to the elders and got married. The honeymoon stage lasted less than one year. In the winter of 2004, my ex-husband met his mistress and started an ongoing affair.

I was so unprepared for what was to come,

In the early part of 2005 after I directed a Sunday morning service, I sat next to my ex-husband on the Church pew. I was happy, all smiles, as I held his hand. I looked over at him and saw he wore a lost look on his face.

Looking back and being older and more experienced, I know that look as one of a person who needs love. At the time I was so happy to be married, going to heaven, able to attend Church again (when you have a child out of wedlock, you were banned from serving until you proved yourself chased), and attending nursing school. I was oblivious to my ex-husband's loneliness. I failed to do what would take me 17 years, two marriages, and countless counseling sessions to learn: I failed to "check in with my spouse."

Imagine how something so simple (yet so vital) can make a world of difference in the ministry of marriage. However, you cannot use tools never given to you.

As I reflect on that marriage, I remember each time my ex-husband would try to express himself I would dismiss it with, "Let us pray about it," or "You simply need to pray more." In a marriage ministry, it is of the utmost importance to *work* towards whatever you are praying for. <u>The truth is the devil does not mind you praying, just as long you do not take it a step too far and work towards that faith!</u>

Oh, we did marital counseling. We saw about three separate marriage counselors. I remember a counselor from a Mega Church in downtown Brooklyn, asked, "Why are trying to save a marriage that is dead?" What I have learned over the years is, most situations in the tertiary stage are almost unsalvable.

Preventative care is always the treatment for any ailment. Failing to be attentive in the ministry of marriage will give the devil an advantage in your union. In this ministry your spouse is your congregant. Your spouse is your God given assignment. There is no disputing in a believer's life, God is first. However, based on the word of God, when you serve your spouse, you honor God (**Hebrew 13:4**). A spouse ignoring or failing to serve the other, is likened unto a Pastor who fails to serve the sheep in his Church. A neglectful Pastor would never be accepted. Why then is it not taken just as seriously when a minister in marriage (spouse) neglects his/her fellow minister (neglected spouse)?

A minister is called to serve. A minister is expected to be flexible and available for service, to love without judgement or favoritism. Ministers of the fivefold ministry and members of the Church all accept these challenging standards as a lifelong call to serve the Lord God. Shouldn't the same be true regarding the calling of spouse-hood? Marriage is the only ministry where a minister (spouse) is willing to place his/her hands on the plow and look back (**Luke 9: 62**).

We stand before the almighty God and vow to serve this office until death. Yet, when attacks us in this area, we high tail out of office without a second thought. The ministry of marriage is held in such high esteem by God, that He models our redemption story after it. The word of God speaks of Jesus being the bridegroom and we (the Church) are His bride (**John 3:29 and Mathews 25:1-13 NKJV**). The wedding ceremony is the equivalent of an ordination ceremony. Both ceremonies are held before a congregation. In both ceremonies, you (the minister) vow to serve the people of God.

You vow to die to self-daily (**Mark 8:34-35 NKJV**). If we hold marriage to the same level as the fivefold ministry, I am convinced that many would be shy from entering into it without great contemplation and guidance. And those who do, would enter well prepared for the call to serve, and be served.

On these next few pages take some time to think about/respond to the prompts 'now.' Later, (six months or more) come back and think about/respond to the same prompts. Note how (if applicable) your responses change.

For Thought: A Call to Serve (Now)

Do you think all problems in marriage can be traced back to a lack of proper premarital preparation?

Is marriage ever the solution to a problem? Why or why not?

Why is it important to do work in a relationship in addition to praying?

How do you minister in marriage?

How can you be certain that you (or someone else) are committed to the ministry of marriage?

"He who finds a wife finds a good thing and obtains favor from the Lord." Proverbs 18:22

"House and wealth are inherited from fathers, but a prudent wife is from the Lord." Proverbs 19:14

"Let marriage be held in honor among all ..." Hebrews 13:4

For Thought: A Call to Serve (Later)

Do you think all problems in marriage can be traced back to a lack of proper premarital preparation?

Is marriage ever the solution to a problem? Why or why not?

Why is it important to do work in a relationship in addition to praying?

How do you minister in marriage?

How can you be certain that you (or someone else) are committed to the ministry of marriage?

"Peace I leave with you; my peace I give you. I do not give to you as the world gives. Do not let your hearts be troubled and do not be afraid." John 14:27

"It is better to live in a corner of the housetop than in a house shared with a quarrelsome wife." Proverbs 21:9

"House and wealth are inherited from fathers,
but a prudent wife is from the Lord." Proverbs 19:14

Chapter Three

A Lack of Knowledge

This book is not an attack on the body of Christ.

I had the honor of interviewing several couples for this book. Their testimonies, my research, and observations serve to illuminate the ministry of marriage which is currently operating under standards that are beneath its value.

In this ministry satan will tempt you to utilize past trauma, self-love, and self-pity to cover pride and destroy your marriage. Pain, trauma, and the 'how dare you do this to me' attitude serve as gateways for the demonic spirit of division to enter your union and dissolve it. The greatest weapon a minister (spouse) can use in such a fight is forgiveness.

Satan is very cunning and deceiving, he will exaggerate your situation, causing you to feel as if you are suffocating in the marriage. Satan will use unforgiveness to cause you to view your spouse as the biggest threat to your life and purpose. You will start thinking suggestive thoughts such as, 'you need to get out, you need a break and next, you need a divorce.'

Poor communication leads to unforgiveness, which in turn causes bitterness and eventually leads to separation and can lead to divorce.

Interview: Lady J. and Mr. Puff

Forgiving and Prioritizing

The first couple, Lady J., and her husband Puff, have been married for the past twenty-one years and are going strong. They are extremely happily married with three children, a thriving ministry called 'Marriage Built to Last' and a women's group called "Prevailing Women." However, if you ask Lady J. and Mr. Puff, they will be the first to tell you, their marriage was not always as it is now. They took me on their journey of love:

Lady J. and Mr. Puff met when she was 16 years old. They attended the same Church, and dated for about two years, before Lady J. would have to leave for college. As Mr. Puff described, the long distance placed a strain on their relationship, and they separated. They reunited one year later, when Lady J. was about 19 years old, became intimate and conceived their first child. As Lady J. explained, "I was terrified and scared." They would eventually confess to their parents and Pastors of the pregnancy.

Lady J. explained her Pastors had no consideration of her age and future, instructed her to marry. Lady J. and Mr. Puff explained had they had pre-marital counseling, proper preparation, it would have saved them four years of heartache.

Five weeks after revealing their pregnancy, the couple were married.

"I was only 19 years old," Lady J. recounted, "not even in adulthood. I had to learn how to be a mom, wife, and manage a household."

The couple further explains that at the time they did not see marriage as a ministry, and they had no clue what life together would be like. They went on to share the first three years of marriage was horrific for them. They did not know how to communicate, balance their finances, or resolve conflicts fairly.

Lady J. and Puff said, "We went to our Pastor and asked him for help."

The pastor promises them a book, and to this date, they still do not have the book. They laugh when they tell that part of the story, although at the time, they felt they were heading towards separation.

They went into tertiary mode and started to read books that could help save their marriage. Lady J. said one book that contributed to saving her marriage was "The Power of a Praying Wife" by Author Stormie Omartian. Lady J. said after reading that book, she understood, she needed to own up to her part in the breakdown of her family. Lady J. said she had a conversation with her husband shortly after reading the book, and as Mr. Puff said, "Things turned around for me when my wife said, if we do not put God first in this marriage, there will not be a marriage."

Out of that conversation, the couple saw their marriage as a ministry they could not give up on. They started to serve in the church and serve each other. When they started to serve as God called them to in their marriage, God elevated them to start the ministry "Marriage Built to Last" which would serve as an anchor to help hold other marriages steady. The couple agreed that an in-depth pre-marital program in the areas of communication, finance, and problem resolution could have saved them years of emotional and psychological pain.

Interview: Mr. & Mrs. Garcon

Patience and Humility

Mr. and Mrs. Garcon have been married for seventeen years and are also going strong. Mr. Garcon was twenty-four years old and Mrs. Garcon twenty-five when they got married. Mrs. Garcon stated that they got married because they were ready for companionship. She states, "God actually revealed to me that he was my husband, so I knew there was no more guessing and that we didn't need to wait any longer." The Garcon's received only three sessions of premarital counseling. The Garcons stated at the time they believed they knew enough and were prepared to be married. However, after they were married, the challenges came. They stated that during those challenging times, they realized that the premarital counseling they received was very superficial. They realized, "there were some things we need to fix ourselves."

The Garcons started tertiary care of their marriage to ensure sustainability. Although they agree preventative care would have helped save time and resources, the couple stated a premarital program that addresses and trains couples on "communication, emotional needs, changing needs, how to fight fair, and how to choose to love when you don't like one another," would have made them feel more prepared.

The oxford dictionary defines humility as a *low view of one's own importance*. A humble person is considerate of others, even above their own needs at times. Humility does not mean you are neglecting yourself. Humility helps a person acknowledge their emotions, thoughts and ideas while seeking to acknowledge, listen to the other person's thoughts and ideas.

Marriage preparation requires patience and humility. If we are honest with ourselves humility mirrors humiliation. There is however a clear difference between the two. The Garcons had to exercise humility to seek knowledge to serve each other.

Satan will use our lack of knowledge of the word of God to set us up on a vicious cycle (**Hosea 4:6 NKJV**). An in-depth premarital counseling will help couples understand that you cannot love anyone if you do not love yourself first (**Mark 12:30-31**). However, the enemy of our soul will do as he did in the garden of Eden - twist the word of God to cause you to sin or forfeit your blessings (**Genesis 3:1**). You will be tempted to only consider others in a misguided effort to please God. Neglecting yourself all the time leads to serious low self-esteem, and confusion. Loving your spouse above yourself is disobedient to Gods words. The enemy can cause you to be frustrated thinking you are doing right putting your spouse first when you are in the wrong. An empty cup can never fill a full one. Marriage requires a spouse to understand balance. Frustration can become bitterness and then, "Why do he/she continue to hurt me without consequences?" becomes a constant thought. Bitterness can set in thereafter and your spouse becomes your hated foe.

In the marriage ministry, the most important rule is submission. In **Genesis 25:3** spouses are called to submit.

Know this: if you trust in God, you will never be put to shame.

On these next few pages take some time to think about/respond to the prompts 'now.' Later, (six months or more) come back and think about/respond to the same prompts. Note how (if applicable) your responses change.

For Thought: A Lack of Knowledge (Now)

Is it easy for you to forgive? Why or why not?

How are emotional needs different from physical needs? Is one more important than the other?

What does humility in a relationship look like? Can humility be humiliating? How so?

What knowledge about marriage (and your spouse) should you arm yourself with?

What does submission look like in a ministry marriage?

The Ministry of Marriage

"What therefore God has joined together, let not man separate." Matthew 19:6

"Above all, keep loving one another earnestly, since love covers a multitude of sins."
1 Peter 4:8

The Ministry of Marriage

"An excellent wife who can find? She is far more precious than jewels."
Proverbs 31:10

For Thought: A Lack of Knowledge (Later)

Is it easy for you to forgive? Why or why not?

How are emotional needs different from physical needs? Is one more important than the other?

What does humility in a relationship look like? Can humility be humiliating? How so?

What knowledge about marriage (and your spouse) should you arm yourself with?

What does submission look like in a ministry marriage?

"And we know that in all things God works for the good of those who love him, who have been called according to his purpose." Romans 8:28

"For as a young man marries a young woman, so shall your sons marry you, and as the bridegroom rejoices over the bride, so shall your God rejoice over you." Isaiah 62:5

"When a man is newly married, he shall not go out with the army or be liable for any other public duty. He shall be free at home one year to be happy with his wife whom he has taken." Deuteronomy 24:5

Chapter Four

Art of War

The word of God will help you to forgive your spouse, humble yourself, and die to self. The word of God reminds spouses they are of one body, one mind, one spirit and one God (**Ephesians 4:4-6**). Married women often find it difficult to take some time off from the family. However, God demands it of you to have a day of rest. Take the plank out of your eyes before removing the plank out of the eyes of someone else. Love yourself before loving your family. An intense premarital program can help spouses to understand effective communication starts in prayer with the Lord God. After the Spirit of all comfort finishes comforting you, then you can comfort your spouse.

The only hope for success in marriage is to learn how to incorporate good and bad moments on the journey and not call it destination. In pre-marital counseling you will gain the tools to die to self-daily. Dying to self in marriage looks different than when you do so in a work setting. In marriage your fellow minister is not your enemy. There is no praying that the east wind takes them away. There is no prayer that you be elevated, and they be put to shame. They are you and you are them, together you both make one. When a member of your physical body is in pain, say your arm for instance, you do not pray God strike it or remove it. You pray God heals your arm that makes up your whole body, so it can regain proper function to perform activity of daily living.

In an equivalent manner, your spouse is the make-up of your life. You must pray for healing and restoration for your spouse, so that your life can be whole, and you both as a unit can perform the daily activities of life. Marriage ministry requires you to constantly pray for and not against your fellow minister.

In early 2023, God had to remind me there is but one accuser of the brethren, satan (**Revelation 12:10 NKJV**). Satan's entire existence is to accuse us before God, highlighting our faults and shortcomings, and attempting to prove our unworthiness of the Lord God's divine protection and blessings (**Job 2:1-6** and **Zechariah 3:1-2 NKJV**). You as a minister of marriage, cannot join in with the accuser of our souls, against your spouse. Do not go before God with arsons of accusations against your spouse, asking God to deal with him/her and close with a proud, "Amen." A body divided against itself simply cannot stand. If you do not plead for your spouse who will?

What I learned in early 2023, and you dear reader must understand, is proper preparation will equip spouses with the tools to sustain a marriage. As the Garcons also mentioned, learn how to love your spouse, even when you do not like your spouse in the now.

In 2023 when I came before God against my spouse, I was requesting His hands of grace and mercy be withheld from my husband! There are so many wives and husbands whose prayers are filled with "see what has been done to me?" and "Lord look what I am suffering with and have to endure?"

I was failing to serve as my husband's ezer. Wives, we are called helpmeet. The Hebrew word for helpmeet is ezer, one who helps, fights for another. The only other reference of an ezer mentioned in the bible is of God defending the children of Israel against their enemies. (Exodus 18:4 and Hosea 13:9). I was saying to the atmosphere, there is no longer a united force in this marriage. Those type of accusatory prayers leave your marriage open to demonic attacks. The enemy strives on division and discord. The word of God states a house united cannot be easily destroyed (**Ecclesiastes 4:9-12**). Stop these damaging prayers in your marriage. Avoid praying about your spouse as the problem. Remember the word of God states, "we do not wrestle against flesh and blood, but against evil, demonic spirits" (**Ephesians 6:12**). The root of a problem in any ministry is mostly spiritual. Attacks (against a ministry) derive from the spiritual realm before it can manifest in the natural world. Pray God open your eyes to the spirit behind the damaging actions taking place, and deal with *that* spirit according to the scriptures.

For example, say your spouse is struggling with poor financial habits. It may be that a spirit of poverty is the root of the problem. Do not pray against your spouse, rather enter your prayer closet, and go to war with the spirit of poverty with the promises of God in His words concerning your finance. Pray God open the affected spouse eyes for need to work towards the faith needed for the situation. In this scenario, the spouse would pray the affected spouse takes a financial literacy class to close the open door for that demonic poverty spirit to have no room to return **(Mathew 12:43-45 NKJV)**.

If you have a spouse who uses manipulation techniques and gaslighting methods to control you, prayer and the word of God can help you as well. If you have a spouse that has a narcissistic personality, your prayer must be aimed at the root of that personality disorder, the Leviathan spirit. **(Psalms 74:14, Isaiah 27:1; Psalm 104:26)**.

Pray and fast against the spirits as a minister would do in any other ministry under attack by the devil. Go into spiritual warfare against the devil, not the person. There are times you will need to call on the elders of the Church and incorporate professional counseling.

War is war and requires force.

On these next few pages take some time to think about/respond to the prompts 'now.' Later, (six months or more) come back and think about/respond to the same prompts. Note how (if applicable) your responses change.

For Thought: The Art of War (Now)

What does self-care mean to you? Do you practice it and if so, how?

What's the difference between a marriage with a destination and a marriage with a journey?

What does it look like to 'join in with the accuser'? How can you prevent this?

Write a sample prayer centered around healing and restoration.

Write sample prayers for a spouse who had financial or manipulation issues that focus on the accuser and not the person.

"An excellent wife is the crown of her husband, but she who brings shame is like rottenness in his bones." Proverbs 12:4

The Ministry of Marriage

"Be on your guard; stand firm in the faith; be courageous; be strong."
1 Corinthians 16:13

"Beloved, let us love one another, for love is from God,
and whoever loves has been born of God and knows God." 1 John 4:7

For Thought: The Art of War (Later)

What does self-care mean to you? Do you practice it and if so, how?

What's the difference between a marriage with a destination and a marriage with a journey?

What does it look like to 'join in with the accuser'? How can you prevent this?

Write a sample prayer centered around healing and restoration.

Write sample prayers for a spouse who had financial or manipulation issues that focus on the accuser and not the person.

The Ministry of Marriage

"Greater love has no one than this; that someone lay down his life for his friends."
John 15:13

The Ministry of Marriage

"Let all that you do be done in love." 1 Corinthians 16:14

"Love and faithfulness meet together; righteousness and peace kiss each other."
Psalm 85:10

Chapter Five

The calling

Spouse-hood is a calling. Everyone is not called to be a wife/husband. The Apostle Paul wrote, it is better for a person not to marry. The unmarried person has more time to pursue the work of God. (**Mathew 19:10-12**, **1 Corinthians 7:1-8**). We all know at least one person who has been single their whole life and is content. Those called to be single simply have *no desire* to have an intimate companion. These willing singles still live a fulfilled life, sharing the joys of life with extended family and friends.

How do you know if you are called to be married? If you are called into the ministry of marriage, you will have a desire to blend and share your life experience with the opposite sex. To blend your life with another is to combine your experiences. Your life experiences are a combination of two thoughts, ideas, and influences always. If you are called to the ministry of marriage your deepest need is to no longer have individual life experiences. You have an innate desire to live an intertwined life, to be one with another person (**Genesis 2:24 NKJV**).

A pre-marital program would help an individual realize if they are called to this life. There are people who dislike the idea of being accountable to another. Ministry of marriage requires a person to give up their individualism. <u>Marriage requires you to even give up full rights to your body.</u> A spouse is in the service ministry. If you are called to be a spouse, you are called to serve. (**1 Corinthians 7:5 NKJV**). God's will in respect to intimacy between husband and wife is held to such a high standard, that God requires a spouse to obtain permission to abstain from sex, even to fast and spend time with God (**1 Corinthians 7:5 NKJV**).

You are called to the ministry of marriage if you find you yearn for physical intimacy. You are called to marry if you must take cold showers to appease your sexual desires. You are called to marry if you must masturbate to appease your flesh. God gave only one way to service your flesh regarding sex and be within His will - through marriage only. (**Hebrews 13: NKJV**). Any sexual intimacy outside of marriage is fornication and is detestable to God.

A pre-marital program will help the body of Christ identify if the calling of marriage is for them. As with the fivefold ministry, <u>if God called a person to marriage, God has equipped them from the beginning of time to have all their spouse will need</u> (**Romans 8:30 NKJV**).

The ministry of marriage affects many factors: community, Church, and souls. There is so much at stake. Therefore, the standards simply cannot continue to be lowered. To continue to allow individuals to enter this ministry without proper preparation is irresponsible.

Interview: L.T. & E.T.

I interviewed a married young woman we will refer to as L.T. At the age of 44 years old, L.T. had been married for 19 years. She got married at the age of twenty-five, after many years of dating her then-boyfriend, E.T.

"I only received four sessions of marital counseling," L.T. explains. She goes on to say, "To tell you the truth I do not recall much about the sessions. I thought that my husband and I were ready for marriage because we were in love."

L.T. revealed that in her four (hour-long) sessions of premarital counseling, no real preparation was offered. L.T. stated that her Pastors did not suggest books to help ensure preparation. According to L.T., the counseling consisted of "just words of wisdom."

After 19 years of marriage, L.T. says she now realizes marriage is a ministry and once entered the devil goes into a never-ending fight to DE-unionize the marriage.

Even though marriage isn't easy, there is still this hope. Jesus said, "Upon this rock I build my church and the gates of hell shall not prevail against it (**Mathew 16:13**). L.T. agrees standards must be raised for marriages to prevail and stated she wishes the Church would develop a program consisting of at least 3-6months of training for a ministry that impacts so many lives. L.T. is now (as many ministers of marriage find themselves) providing tertiary care for her marriage. L.T. agrees, preventative care would have been best.

I mentioned in previous chapters I am on my third marriage. It is here, God gave me the revelation that marriage was a ministry. And although I am called to this ministry, I have taken it for granted and assumed all that was required was love and to be equally yoked.

I was young when I entered my first marriage and received no marriage counseling. I entered marriage in the summer of 2004, was separated by

2006, and divorced in 2010. I was not prepared on how to manage conflict. Adultery is a hard hit on a marriage; however, I now understand, conflict resolution skills (requires training) can help prevent divorce.

In 2010 (my ex and I started dating 2008), after one session of premarital counseling, I made my second attempt at marriage (still not understanding this was a ministry). I remember the Pastor saying, "This is going to be a faithful mess." And he was right. I separated in 2012 and divorced in 2017. My ex-husband could not hold a steady job, we were struggling financially, and I had to move into public housing to be able to afford a roof over our heads. I was not prepared for how financial strain can affect a marriage.

With my current marriage, my husband and I received three sessions of pre-marital counseling of the same caliber. In this marriage, I realized communication skills and the requirement of dying to self is one of the key factors for its survival.

I am convinced one of the reasons marriages are so easy for people to jump in and out of is because the standard of entry is too low. There is not a person before they enter a profession who does not stop to count the cost. Whether it be a certificate or degree program, you look at the curriculum requirements and length of training to see if it will be worth the effort.

To drive a car a person requires months of training including a driving test. This is required due to the potential harm and even death an ill prepared driver can cause to another. Marriage is just as dangerous in the hands of an ill-prepared person. Statistics have proven how divorce impacts lives, communities, and Churches. The bar must be raised by which a person is issued a marriage license. I am not calling to hinder people from getting married. I am calling for change in the requirement process - especially in the body of Christ.

On these next few pages take some time to think about/respond to the prompts 'now.' Later, (six months or more) come back and think about/respond to the same prompts. Note how (if applicable) your responses change.

For Thought: The Calling (Now)

Do you have a desire to blend your life? What does that look like?

Do you have an innate desire to live an intertwined life? What does that look like?

Are you capable of surrendering your body to your spouse? How do you know?

Do you yearn for physical intimacy in a sexual manner?

Do you feel equipped to enter the ministry of marriage? How do you know?

"For as high as the heavens are above the earth, so great is his love for those who fear him." Psalm 103.11

"I love the Lord, for he heard my voice; he heard my cry for mercy.
Because he turned his ear to me, I will call on him as long as I live." Psalm 116:1-2

"Give thanks to the God of heaven. His love endures forever." Psalm 136:26

For Thought: The Calling (Later)

Do you have a desire to blend your life? What does that look like?

Do you have an innate desire to live an intertwined life? What does that look like?

Are you capable of surrendering your body to your spouse? How do you know?

Do you yearn for physical intimacy in a sexual manner?

Do you feel equipped to enter the ministry of marriage? How do you know?

"The Lord is gracious and compassionate, slow to anger and rich in love."
Psalm 145:8

"He heals the brokenhearted and binds up their wounds." Psalm 147

The Ministry of Marriage

"For the Lord takes delight in his people; he crowns the humble with victory."
Psalm 149:4

Chapter Six

Putting on the full armor for the fight.

In **Ephesians 6:11-13**, Paul calls for believers of Jesus Christ to put on the full armor of God to fight against the devil. One of those armor is the sword of the spirit, which is the word of God. The word of God teaches us people perish due to lack of knowledge (**Hosea 4:6 NKJV**). Having knowledge is one thing, but you must *understand* what you profess to know. (**Proverb 4:7**). After understanding you must learn how to *apply*. It is the application process that requires training (**James 1:5**).

How can the Church help reduce divorce rates, save lives, and improve the quality of life for the body of Christ? I propose a three to six months pre-marital training program. In this preventive approach, the Church can ensure that the individuals coming to them to enter the ministry of marriage are prepared for what the office of marriage will demand of them.

The pre-marital course outline should consist of the following classes:

Emotional Intelligence Class: "Emotional intelligence is the ability or skill to be intelligent about your own and those of others, which includes "emotional quotient, the ability to recognize, decern and manage emotions."

Having emotional intelligence helps a person "extend from controlling your emotions internally when dealing with yourself and externally in interpersonal relationships." This skill helps you "pay attention to your emotions and the emotions of those around you while naming and labeling these correctly and use the emotional information gathered from this exercise to respond appropriately."

In this class the engaged couple will relate to each other on an intellectual level. God requires this level of emotional intelligence to the degree He will not answer a husband's prayer if the husband does not deal with his wife with intelligence (**1 Peter 3:7 NKJV**). In marriages there are times when you will be angry. Anger is a natural emotion: however, it can become detrimental if you allow it to linger. The word of God require you should not go to bed angry. Going to bed angry risks opening the doors to the enemy to have access to destroy your marriage (**Ephesians 4:26-27**, **Psalm 4:4-8 NKJV**).

"Anger is a healthy release. It takes an enormous amount of energy to hold anger inside, which may cause fatigue, boredom, and physical illness. If you release your anger appropriately, you may find that you develop healthier relationships." (**ANGER MANAGEMENT FOR THE TWENTY-FIRST CENTURY, ANTHONY FIORE, PHD AND ARI NOVICK, PHD.**)

Conflict Resolution Class: in this class the intends will learn skills to manage the problems of marriage. All marriages have problems. All couples argue. It is the way a problem and/or argument is managed that will ensure healthy outcomes. One key factor in conflict resolution is humility.

"There is nothing so natural to man, nothing so insidious, and hidden from our sight, nothing so difficult and dangerous, as pride." **(HUMILITY BY ANDREW MURRAY, 1982, PG19)**

"All the wretchedness in this world has its origin in what this cursed, hellish pride-either our own, or that of others-has brought us. All wars and bloodshed among the nations, all selfishness and suffering, all ambitions and jealousy, all broken hearts, and embittered lives, with all daily unhappiness are result of this same wicked pride." **(EMOTIONAL INTELLIGENCE BY BRANDON GOLEMAN, 2020, SECOND EDITION, PG.24)**

Humility helps a person argue without casting blame and considering the other person, feelings, thoughts, and ideas. Satan would like nothing better than for a person to enter marriage thinking it is their way or the highway. The thought that you are always right, and others are wrong, is not of God. Selfish thinking will cause you to have unhealthy arguments where you seek to be right rather than seeking an amicable resolution. Seeking to be right in arguments brings shame and guilt to your spouse which is a weapon of the enemy not a grace of God.

"Excessive guilt and sorrow can only lead to depression, despair, and defeat. Sometimes it led to destruction: Christian has been known to commit suicide in order to escape satanic accusation." **(THE STRATEGY OF SATAN: HOW TO DETECT & DEFEAT HIM, BY WARREN W. WIERSBE, 1979, PG79)**

Even in arguments a person must do it with love, respect, and great consideration for the other person (**2 Corinthians 2:7-11 NKJV**).

Communications Class: It is said that words are only seven percent of communication. Communication is not just opening your mouth and allowing words to come forth. A person getting ready to spend 24 hours with another person for the rest of their life needs to, at the most, master communication and at the very least, train in the art of communications.

"Humans seem to have developed a certain kind of communications to a rare pitch of sophistication. Our commend of the spoken language is extraordinary; but just as impressive are our abilities to read facial impressions, tone of voice, and gesture." **(IMPROVE YOUR COMMUNICATION SKILLS, HOW TO BUILD TRUST, BE HEARD AND COMMUNICATE WITH CONFIDENCE, BY ALAN BARKER, FIFTH EDITION 2019, PAGE 1)**

Effective communication is the foundation of all successful marriages. The ability to face every other challenge in your marriage will be based on how well you can communicate effectively.

WARRING!!!

Do not enter marriage without learning this skill. Communication is not (I repeat) just speaking words.

Effective communication can help you have a give and take relationship. "When a couple agrees to meet any of each other's emotional needs, whether it's sex or family commitment, the way they go about it must be in the best interest of both spouses, not just one." **(GIVE & TAKE, THE SECRET TO MARITAL COMPATIBILITY, BY WILLARD F. HARLEY, JR., 1996 PAGE 155)**

Effective communication can help manage unrealistic expectations in your marriage. When you have set up in your mind the way your marriage should be, based on your culture, upbringing and or ideals, that can create chaos in your marriage.

"We have a picture of the perfect partner, but we marry an imperfect person. Then we have two options. Tear up the picture and accept the person or tear up the person and accept the picture." **(WHEN BAD THINGS HAPPENS TO GOOD MARRIAGES, BY LES AND LESLIE PARROTT, 2001, PAGE 33)**

"Without conversation, the warm atmosphere and the deep physical relationship each partner needs could never be maintained!" **(His Needs Her Needs, Building an affair-proof Marriage by Willard F. Harley, Jr, 11th edition February 2005, page 68)**

Financial Literacy Class: In a pre-marital program, the intended can develop skill to identify their money habits as well as their fiancée's money habits. Learning how you and your fiancée view money is vital to maintaining a healthy marriage. It is during this class you will communicate and decide on joint or separate accounts. It is during the pre-marital phase you should have a clear understanding if there will be one or two working spouses.

During this class spouses will come to a clear understanding on whether tithing and support of charity and Church is going to be a principle in their marriage (**Mathew 6:21**). During this class it is important to be transparent. Discussions on how many bank accounts and monies each person has should be shared. If there are any doubts on forgotten accounts you can do a search online, such as searching the US savings bond database.

"When you are searching for these systems, be smart. You need to use every advantage, which means you should list all names by which you have been known." **(FREE MONEY, "THEY" DON'T WANT YOU TO KNOW ABOUT BY KEVIN TRUDEAU'S, 2009, PAGE 26)** This proactive measure can help save years of hard lessons and pain. A financially stable marriage does not happen by chance. *"The power of choice, not chance, was what made the difference."* **(START WHERE YOU ARE BY CHRIS GARDNER, 2009, PAGE 27)**

Parenting & Intimacy Class (*optional*): Too often couples get married and lose their sexual desire for one another. After marriage, work, kids, and other factors of life tend to be placed on the priority list and our spouse's physical needs are placed on the back burner. Not meeting your spouse's needs can be fatal for your marriage. Undermining each other in front of the children is another damaging behavior to have in your marriage.

"Develop a couple-centered, not a child-centered, relationship. This is the first time in your relationship that you will have to choose who really comes first. Starting right here and now, determine that the couple comes before the children. The order of priorities must be God first, marriage second, and children third, if you want your marriage to continue to grow stronger through each of the consecutive stages." (**Childproofing your Marriage: keeping your marriage a priority during parenting years by Dr. Debbie L. Cherry, 2004, page 176**)

There are couples who feel guilty placing their marriage before their children, however, you must remember, your spouse is expected to be with you until death. Your children will leave you to start a life of their own (**Genesis 2:24**).

On these next few pages take some time to think about/respond to the prompts 'now.' Later, (six months or more) come back and think about/respond to the same prompts. Note how (if applicable) your responses change.

For Thought: Putting On the Full Armor for The Fight (Now)

How do you manage your emotions? How do you manage the emotions of others? What areas need improvement?

How do you resolve conflict? What areas need improvement?

What type of communicator are you? What areas need improvement?

Describe your financial skills? What areas need improvement?

Describe your parenting style? What areas need improvement?

What does Intimacy mean to you? Are there areas that you can improve?

"You make known to me the path of life; you will fill me with joy in your presence,
with eternal pleasures at your right hand." Psalm 16:11

"May these words of my mouth and this meditation of my heart
be pleasing in your sight, Lord, my Rock and my Redeemer." Psalm 19:14

"Be still before the Lord and wait patiently for him; do not fret when people succeed in their ways, when they carry out their wicked schemes." Psalm 37:7

For Thought: Putting On the Full Armor for The Fight (Later)

How do you manage your emotions? How do you manage the emotions of others? What areas need improvement?

How do you resolve conflict? What areas need improvement?

What type of communicator are you? What areas need improvement?

Describe your financial skills? What areas need improvement?

Describe your parenting style? What areas need improvement?

What does Intimacy mean to you? Are there areas that you can improve?

"Teach me your way, Lord, that I may rely on your faithfulness; give me an undivided heart, that I may fear your name." Psalm 86:11

The Ministry of Marriage

"But I will not take my love from him, nor will I ever betray my faithfulness."
Psalm 89:33

"Praise the Lord, my soul, and forget not all his benefits." Psalm 103:2

Epilogue

An Appeal to the Church

The word of God says in **Isaiah 59:19**, "when the enemy comes in like a flood, the spirit of the lord will raise up a standard against him.) We as the Church must rise to that standard. The flood of divorce waves is hitting the Church, it cannot be left to sweep over the Church like a tsunami. The Church is doing a phenomenal job at tertiary care: there are countless marital retreats, seminars, and marriage counseling aimed at helping to rebuild broken marriages. However, I believe in this dispensation God is calling on the Church to take action to *prevent* the problems from developing. The divorce problem can no longer be viewed as an individual's problem. It is a systemic problem at this point.

Divorce not only impacts families and communities, but it also affects every part of the Church, from the finances to members' attendance and worship quality. Two-income households because of divorce now become a one-income household. The tithes decrease or are stopped altogether. The members start to miss Church related to increased responsibility or a second job to pay the bills. This now divorcee, comes to Church hurt and broken, heavy in their spirit cannot worship. Divorce is not a one-person problem; divorce is like a disease that spreads.

Churches must raise the bar. If a system does not work, then that system needs revamping. Too long have people been allowed to jump into this vital commitment unprepared. Two or three sessions on "how you guys met" just will not cut it anymore. The Church needs to develop a pre-marital program on topics that are globally known to be the destroyer of marriages. The pre-marital program is not a means to control people's decisions. However, it is a way to help ensure that the parties involved will make informed decisions.

Marriage may not be viewed as a vital ministry because many are called into it; however, this is precisely the reason the Church must raise the standard to ensure its success. Many are called to the ministry of marriage because it holds one of the greatest of commandments, be fruitful and multiply. Marriage ensures people will multiply in God's glory. As with the great commission, all are called to spread the good news once they have received it. The news of the love of our Lord and savior Jesus Christ is too great to be left to one office. All must go and tell of the love of God (**Mark 16:15**).

Even with new converts, it is the leaders of the Church, once they are saved, to ensure discipleship classes such as bible study, prayer session, and quality sermons are provided for the converts hearing. The same must be true for marriage-minded individuals. The leaders of the Church must take aggressive action toward this demonic spirit of divorce. God has shown us the best way to cast this demon out is through prayer, fasting, and raising up the standard.

This will not be easy to develop a premarital program. However, nothing we do to advance the kingdom of God is ever easy. Yet, we know we can do all things through Christ who strengthen us (**Philippians 4:13**).

This program does not have to be costly to the Church. All that needs to be done is replace the three sessions with three months classes with touch points of subjects mentioned in previous chapters and/or more based on each Church assessment. <u>Marriage is not the solution for life issues like pre-marital pregnancy, loneliness, homelessness, immigration fraud, among other things.</u> Marriage is a ministry mirrored by the relationship God has with the Church of Jesus Christ. The call to marriage must be honored and prepared for equally to the call to office of the fivefold ministries.

We are the Church; the gates of hell can never prevail over us (**Matthew 16:18**). I appeal to the individual reading this book, if you are married and going through a rough time, please reach out to leaders. Do not be ashamed. Your marriage does not have to end in divorce. There is help for you and your spouse. If you are reading this and are engaged or considering marriage, please make it a point to take classes in the areas highlighted in this book with your fiancée. It will serve no purpose if you take these classes alone. (*The engaged couple must participate in the program together via means that apply.*) The point of this approach is to ensure both parties have a clear understanding and agree on how they will as a unit address these areas in their journey together, forever. Forever is a long time to enter a covenant and be unprepared.

I pray the ministry of marriage in Church today is not set up for failure and that the standards are high - as God mandated.

Now, let us rise to meet it!

Thank you

About the Author

Mirielle Archange Gordon was born in 1980 in Port-au-Prince Haiti. She migrated to the great country of the United States of America in 1985. Mirielle was born out of wedlock to parents who believed in God and made sure she and her four brothers attended Church regularly. However, although the family believed in God, Mirielle was never taught to serve God.

Growing up, Mirielle was a witness to marriages destroyed by affairs, selfishness, financial abuse, physical and emotional abuse. Later in life her mother confessed to a curse placed in their bloodline:

"No woman in the family will remain married. Those who do stay married will live separate lives. Only God will ever break the curse."

At the age of thirteen, Mirielle gave her life to Jesus Christ in a small local Pentecostal Church, which was made up of over 75% women and children. Here she learned to serve God. One year later, at the age of fourteen, Mirielle was baptized.

Twice divorced and currently married for three years, Mirielle witnessed damage firsthand (and at a distance) of what divorce and broken family structures can do to families, communities, and future generations. The brokenness of divorce serves as a motivating factor for her desire to offer a vaccine to help the body of Christ fight a great and overlooked pandemic – divorce.

"I hope to be among a great body of believers called by God," Mirielle proclaims, "to rebuild and/or build strong families, communities, and future generation by restructuring the Church's view on marriage."

The author founded an online support group for women entitled My Sisters Keepers. She recently opened a support group for wives, entitled

Wives Waiting Room for women going through hardships in their marriage.

The mother of five children (four living): Christina, Patrick, Abigail, and Malachi currently reside in Georgia where she has been a registered nurse for more than 15 years. Mirielle attends a Mega Church in Georgia where she serves in the medical and praise and worship ministries. She also serves remotely as a welcoming team member at a well-known international Church in Florida.

Mirielle recently earned a certificate in Cognitive Behavioral Therapy and is enrolled in Liberty University pursuing a major in Psychology - Christian Family Counseling.

An Author's Declaration:

To YOU who read this I declare your marriage is/will be blessed, of the Lord,

and no demonic spirit, or person, will come between you and your spouse.

I declare you are anointed to be who God has called you to be,

through the power of the Holy Spirit of the Living God.

You are equipped from the beginning of time

to be a wife/husband to your spouse.

In Jesus Christ name,

Amen.

References:

(https://dictionary.cambridge.org)

(https://study.com/learn/lesson/convenant-biblical.com)

(https://www.merriam-webster.com/dictionary/pre-) (https://www.merriam-webster.com/dictionary/pre-

(https://www.merriam-webster.com/dictionary/pre-

(https//www.ncbi.nlm.nih.gov/pmc/articles/pmc4012696/)

(https://www.ncbi.nlm.nih.gov/pmc/articles/PMC4012696/)

(Experience of Child-Parent Separation and Later Risk of Violent Criminality (https://www.ncbi.nlm.nih.gov/pmc/articles/PMC6057277/)

(https://georgia.govapply-marriage-license)

(https://dphgeorgia.gov/WIC/wic-news-alert)

(Emotional Intelligence by Brandon Goleman,2020, second edition, pg.7)

(Anger Management for Twenty-first Century, by Anthony Fiore, PhD and Ari Novick, PhD, 2005, pg. ix)